A Mirror to Nature

A Mirror to Nature

Poems About Reflection

Jane Yolen

Photographs by Jason Stemple

WORDSONG

HONESDALE, PENNSYLVANIA

Wordsong
An Imprint of Boyds Mills Press, Inc.
815 Church Street
Honesdale, Pennsylvania 18431
Printed in China

Library of Congress Cataloging-in-Publication Data

Yolen, Jane.
  A mirror to nature : poems about reflection / poetry by
Jane Yolen ; photographs by Jason Stemple. — 1st ed.
    p. cm.
  ISBN 978-1-59078-624-6 (alk. paper)
  1. Water—Optical properties—Juvenile poetry.
  2. Children's poetry, American. I. Stemple, Jason,
ill. II. Title.
  PS3575.O43M57 2009
  811'.54—dc22

                                    2008031760

First edition
The text of this book is set in 14-point Wilke Roman.

10 9 8 7 6 5 4 3 2 1

"To hold, as 'twere,
the mirror up to nature ..."

Hamlet, act 3, scene 2,
by William Shakespeare

To those wonderful reflections,
my twin granddaughters,
Caroline and Amelia
—*J.Y.*

For my beautiful wife, Joanne
—*J.S.*

Contents

On Reflection: A Note from the Author

The first mirror was water: puddles, pools, lakes, quiet rivers. Humankind did not make actual mirrors of glass until relatively late in our shared history. Mirrors from ancient Greece and Rome, for example, were disks of polished metal. Glass mirrors were perfected during the Middle Ages.

When Jason was photographing reflections in nature, water was the element that drew his eye, not only for its reflective qualities but because the doubled image makes a fascinating pattern. Whether it's a strange alien raccoon with four ears and four eyes, a coyote against a snowy bank, or an egret's seemingly extra-long legs that bend at impossible angles, the reflection offers us something new to look at.

Something new to look at: that is another way of defining the word *reflection*. To reflect on something is to give it a deep and different look, to think about it in a new way. So, linger over these photos, contemplate the poems, see if together or separately they make you think again, make *you* reflect.

—*Jane Yolen*

Swimming with Raccoons

One raccoon, halved, whole,
Doubled, wet, worried, swimming,
Two eyes, four eyes, in the cold,
Hair above, below, needs trimming.

One raccoon, divided, twinned,
Angry, soaking, snarled, and snarling,
Two ears, four ears hear the wind.
On dry land the children's darling.

As adorable as they look, wild raccoons should be left alone. They can bite and often carry all kinds of diseases, including rabies.

Raccoon

Wood Stork

How the Wood Stork Population Might Grow

How to double your population?
Stand in water smooth as glass.
This is not mere speculation.
Check the wood storks by the grass.

I count seven in the group,
But by viewing their reflection,
Double up the wood stork troop—
A population resurrection.

*The only stork species that breeds in North America, the
wood stork is on the endangered species list. Only about
five thousand breeding pairs exist in the country, a result
of extreme weather conditions and a loss of habitat.*

Jaws x 2 x 80

Because
of jaws,
I stay out
of the river.

One pair's
a scare,
the other—
full shiver.

One pair
is real,
and one
a reflection.

But I'll never
give either
a closer
inspection.

The American alligator has between seventy and eighty teeth. When one falls out, another grows in its place.

Deer

The Deer Reflects Himself

Oh dear, oh deer,
don't stand
reflecting.
Run
on your swift feet.
A deer that stays
too long
reflecting
is a deer called
meat.

*In some places, deer herds have grown so
large they are considered a nuisance.*

Moorhen's Mirror

Such a quirky
water bird.
Its duplication
is absurd,
reminding us
that nature's sense
of humor's strange—
and quite immense.

The moorhen was originally called a marsh hen,
after its habitat.

Common Moorhen

Snail

How Speeds the Snail

The only way the snail
Can multiply its pace
Is when its numbers double
Upon a water race.

Carefully reflecting,
It figures how to go.
The twinning snails come quickly.
Originals are slow.

*Snails belong to the class Gastropod, which is
second only to insects in its total number of
species. A snail can glide on its single foot,
but it's slow going.*

Spoonbill Haiku

The princess of birds.
Her only competition
Is her reflection.

*The roseate spoonbill may be the princess of birds,
but it's often mistaken for a flamingo, the queen of
fliers, because they are both pink. But one look at
the spatulate beak of the spoonbill should be a
dead giveaway.*

Roseate

Spoonbill

Cockle

A Solitary Cockle

O to be a solitary cockle,
Sitting silent in reflection,
Somewhat open to the moment,
Somewhat into introspection.

Never needing to be acting,
Never having to be hammy,
Just a solitary bivalve
In the water, silent … clammy.

*Cockles, often mistaken for clams, are members
of the Cardiidae family. Like clams, they have
two "valves," or shells, connected by a hinge joint.
Cockles have a foot with which they can burrow
in the sand.*

Bottle/Frog

As if he thinks he's on a log,
This perplexing little frog
Has popped up on a thrown-out bottle.
What does this mean? Perhaps a lotle.

And his mirror twin, that clown,
Floats in water upside down,
But on a bottle, not a log.
An equally perplexing frog.

You see—a log breaks down at last
While a bottle holds on fast
To its shape down through the years.
As for that log? It disappears.

A for effort? F for skill?
Make of these frogs what you will.
Silly frogs, both on parade
On bottles that just won't degrade.

Scientists consider frogs an "indicator species," which means they serve as a warning when something is wrong in an ecosystem. Since 1980, more than one hundred species of amphibians have disappeared around the world.

Coyote Landscape

For a moment, you are as still
As the roots, rocks, snow.
Only the water runs fast,
As fast as you, when you go

Whipping the wind, blazing the trail,
Following the panting prey.
But now, for a moment, you stand statue still
Reflecting on the day.

A running coyote can reach speeds of up to
forty-three miles per hour. It often hunts in pairs.

Red-Tail Sail

A small pleasure yacht is the sloop.
It has two sails hung out aft and fore.
When the sloop's on the sea,
With its sails running free,
It's better out there than on shore.

The big red-tail drum is the same.
It has moves in the water galore.
But when it is crabbing,
And dinner it's grabbing,
It looks as if rigged aft and fore.

So the fisherman out after drum
Knows that fishing is never a chore.
His careful inspection
Finds red tail's reflection,
And—*pop!*—he's got one redfish more!

The redfish, or red drum, lives in saltwater creeks, often swimming with its head down, rooting around for crabs. That causes its tail to lift out of the water, making it easy for fishermen to spot.

S n o w y   E g r e t

*Snowy egrets stand
twenty-two to twenty-six
inches high—except when
they are reflected in water.*

Crazy Legs

How it fools the eye,
Reflection.

The egret's
Stark perfection
Now marked
By strange bisection.
So bent, this odd
Direction
Demands a new
Inspection.

Crazy legs.

Does our perception
Need a
Surgical correction
Or perhaps
A new injection
Of common
Introspection
Topped by
Tranquil
Recollection?